Handprints on the Womb

Poetry by Theodore Richards

Forward by Brian Swimme

PORTLAND • OREGON
INKWATERPRESS.COM

www.inkwaterpress.com

ISBN-13 978-1-59299-442-7
ISBN-10 1-59299-442-3

Publisher: Inkwater Press

Printed in the U.S.A.
All paper is acid free and meets all ANSI standards for archival quality paper.

1

To my wife, Arianne, whose presence in my life is all the poetry I need.

Acknowledgments

Thank you to my daughter, Cosima Sing Teifi Richards, for teaching me that I am a poet; to my brother, for his courage; to Brian Swimme and the PCC department at the California Institute of Integral Studies, where both my teachers and colleagues gave me immeasurable inspiration; to Matthew Fox and YELLAWE, where my students have taught me far more wisdom than I could ever teach them; to the late Sifu Tony Roberts, my Bagua Zhang teacher, for teaching me the mysteries of the Tao; to Sue Duncan and everyone at the Children's Center in Chicago; to the Tibetan monks who cared for me when I had altitude sickness, the kind strangers who shared fruit with me in Mozambique and Iran, and the people on the margins, everywhere, who have a wisdom toward which I only aspire; to Maxwell Mponda, my partner in Zimbabwe, with hope that you are alright; to my poet-teachers, Dante, Rilke, Whitman, Dylan Thomas, Mary Oliver, Alice Walker, Wendell Berry, Rumi, Ibn 'Arabi, Hip Hop, and the Romantics.

Thank you to the trees, the mountains and the sea; to the stream behind my house in east Oakland; thank you to the stars; and thank you to the Universe, for the 13.7 billion year gestation process which allowed for the birth of this project.

Contents

Forward

The poetry and photography of Theodore Richards take us into the edge of the universe, where "edge" is understood not so much as a location in space but rather as an event in time, a realm in which a billion year past collides with a wavefront of possibilities coming to us freshly from the future, moment after moment. At this edge, he tells us, we "are giving birth to ourselves, giving birth to the fruit of summer's possibility". It is at this edge that we are "being born into a new womb." The physicist Richard Feynman offered a related theory when he insisted that in order to conceptualize reality at its most fundamental level, one needs to think not only of particles moving forward from the past through a series of causes; one must also think of anti-particles moving *backwards* in time, from a future toward the present.

I cite this theory from quantum physics in order to highlight the multidimensional nature of "Handprints on the Womb." Like Dante Alighieri, Theodore Richards' poems arise out of a synthesis of personal experience and scientific understanding of the universe, and they aim at speaking directly to the ancient questions of meaning. Though Dante based his vision on the medieval science deriving from Aristotle and St. Thomas, and Richards begins instead with twenty-first century evolutionary science, both are committed to the central challenge of cosmological poetry, which is to provide a whole story of where we have come from and why we are here in the midst of this universe drama.

Theodore Richards, with his poetic vision, takes us on an epic journey through the hell of Cook County Jail, the Africa of Mozambique, and the endlessness of the Pacific Ocean. It is his journey and it is our journey. It is humanity's journey and though it necessarily includes the misery of cruelty and oppression, there is a wisdom at work as well. A cry of compassion and outrage haunts these poems. Things could be so very different. We wandered away from our African origins so many millennia ago, and though we have often become lost and confused, the universe leaves clues everywhere. A father glances at his daughter and sees "The stars in her flesh/The seas in her tears." A new beginning is possible, a new feeling for the interconnectedness of all things is before us. Richards takes us on a journey into the edge of the universe which is the edge of the human being which is the edge of God. Here is a journey to that place where, as Virgil instructed Dante, the human gives birth to the world, and where, as Richards instructs us, we can "dream a world to life", we can "live the love that burns."

Brian Swimme
California Institute of Integral Studies

Preface

I didn't know I was a poet until my daughter was born. That day, I wrote a poem. Then I began to go back through my old journals hidden in closets, pieces of paper tucked away in books. Napkins in the corner of my desk. I excavated poems from prose. And there it was.

Handprints on the Womb is loosely modeled on Dante's *Commedia*, consisting of the realms of *Inferno*, *Purgatorio*, and *Paradiso*. For Dante, this was the three-fold structure of his world. I choose them not to advocate a return to the medieval cosmology, but to suggest that our work—with the help of the poet, the artist and the mystic—is to participate meaningfully in our world, however we conceive of it.

The poet's job is not merely to write, but to create our world through the imagination. This is done not so much with proclamations about universal truths but by living one's own personal story as fully and deeply as one can, allowing, one hopes, others to see their own unique story expressed in another. We write to express our felt sense of connection to one another and to the Universe and hope that others will have compassion for what we have felt. I promise the reader nothing but the intensity of the feelings I convey, the authenticity of the experiences that has given rise to them. Compassion is lived in this way, and we surely cannot live without it.

Unlike Dante, I write these poems from a modern perspective, which brings with it both advantages and disadvantages. While it requires a great deal more creative energy to find the felt sense of connection to my world that was so central to the medieval mind, I also have the advantage of many great insights unimagined by my ancestors. For instance, we understand time now in a new, dynamic way. We live in a Universe, according to today's science, in which time must be accounted for in ways never imagined in Dante's era. Time and space are intimately linked; a contemporary picture of the cosmos, therefore, cannot be one of static layers of space, as Dante's was, but of dynamic space-time, represented by past (*inferno*), present (*purgatorio*), and future (*paradiso*). Both past and future is present in each of us in the present, expressed through the unique vision of the poet. And just as Dante's work represented a world that can only be understood as a whole, a whole that is reflected in the soul of the individual, these poems are an expression of my own experience of the Universe in its fullness each moment—the past, the story of its becoming, is present in my own body, at this moment; and the future is present in my ability to imagine and create that which is not yet present.

To give birth to a novel mythology—"a new story" in the words of Thomas Berry—requires not only ideas about our world, but deeply felt relationships within it. Science and philosophy requires the mythteller, the poet, to bring their ideas to life. While I present Dante as the archetypal philosopher-poet, creating his world, there is no individual who can do this work alone. Collectively, we sit around the fire, creating our world with our poems and songs. Collectively, our hands touch the edge of our womb-world. There is much that is missing from this work considering the lofty goals I have set... I humbly leave this work to the reader.

Inferno

Salimmo suso, ei primo ed io secondo,
Tanto ch'io vidi delle cose belle
Che porta il ciel, per un pertugio tondo;
E quindi uscimmo a riveder le stelle.[1]

Dante, *Inferno*, Canto xxxiv, 136-139[2]

---

1 ∞ "We climbed up, he first and I second,/ so that I saw among the beautiful things/ which Heaven bears, through a round opening/ and from there we went forth, once more, to see the stars." [translation mine]
2 Dante Alighieri, *The Inferno of Dante Alighieri* (London: J.M. Dent & Sons, 1946) p.390

Inferno: The Journey into the Soul

Fire
I write these words
With a mind, a hand
A body
On fire
A soul is born
And at its center
Is a cosmos
Of memories
The past
Burning in my depths
A soul
A body
A Universe
Birthed in fire
Dark Matter
Is my Dark Mother,
I see her in deep in space
Burning
In my heart.
The primordial fireball
The stars,
The fire of
My ancestors
Dance around the fire
Dance around the Sun
Dance around my soul
On fire
My Ancestors,
The stars.

"A Child was Murdered"

[For Girl X]

A child was murdered today
By children
But this one had always fought
To unlearn what she had been taught
So she sought flowers where none grew
Powers, no one knew
She fought.
Brought into a loveless world
She loved.

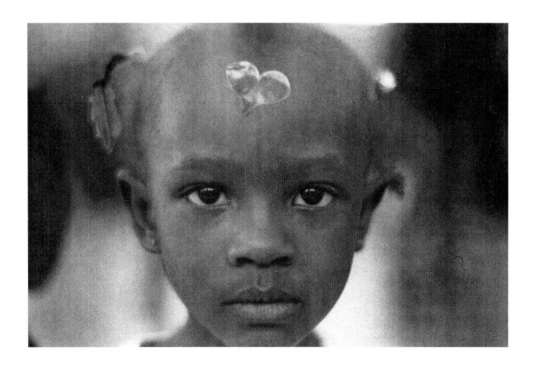

October 1998, Chicago

"They Came One by One"

[For Ollie]

They came one by one
To a childless mother
Who took them in.

The little ones came shaking
Skinny
Addicted
Drugs running through their veins.

The older ones had lived in the streets
Abandoned cars
Basements
And if they were lucky
Projects

They had been cheated
The heaven of the womb that is our right
From conception
Had been desecrated,
Profaned
Polluted.
They left that Hellish Heaven for another Hell
Of strange places,
Strange men
Of abandonment

They loved their mother, still
She was once beautiful
I am told
Until she lost her hair
Her teeth
So much weight, and pride.

Almost wasted away
Scratched her face until it left deep scars.
Deep scars.
But a child's love can see into the past
And she remains beautiful
Even a mother with deep scars

I drive through streets blacked out
Blocked off by gangs
Forced to turn around
Teenaged girls lead the little ones
Across the street
I hear gunshots, sirens, calling
Whom?

I wonder:
Can the men in suits
From towers that scrape the heavens—
Polluting, profaning this world that should be our womb—
Hear too?
Do they wonder how this could happen
In the land of the free and the home
Of the brave?
Or do they just swell up
With patriotic pride
At the sirens red glare
Bullets bursting in air
Bursting dreams—silently,
But no less violently—
In despair?

1999, Chicago

"Bloodstained"

Hands covered with blood
I stand.
i stand
waiting
For it to dry I
Cry
From my blood-shot-red-eye
Tears, smeared across my face.

I am bloodstained.
Hands tinted red
Fingertips
Brownyellow between my first two fingers,
Where roaches squeezed
My eyes red, from too much to drink last night
Up, too early in the morning.

I am stained
I wear my past lives on my presence—
Passed lives that include the constant rebirths within this one—
Worn like a bloodyscarlet letter
Somewhere between whoiam and whoiwas
Between the skin I can never shed
And clothes I can so easily remove before bed
A burden I was not born with
But cannot die without

I can leave
Will leave
Must leave
But I cannot leave myself

I stand before this bravenewworld
Stained
Marked
Blood on my hands
Rejecting my past
Rejected by my future
Scrubbing my skin
In the present
Until it bleeds

Chicago, February 1999

"I am"

I am;

I am the dark matter of my dark mother, burning deep in space;

I am the salty ocean of my tears,

      tears shed for a world of possibility and despair;

I am the story of my ancestors, and the imagination of my daughter;

I am memories of the long journeys, of stories told in darkness by the fire,

      and in the moonlight;

I am the cave paintings, and the handprints on the womb;

I am being born each moment,

      new and fresh.

I am the parched Earth, the crying skies;

I am Imagination,

      tapestry of humanity's yearnings for the future,

      depth of my own uniqueness.

And I am the dying Earth,

      crying for the memory of the gifts she gave us,

      of the struggles of my mothers.

October 2008, Oakland

"Lost"

In the greenest of forests
I am lost among the trees of life.
Entangled in questioning vines
Searching, seeking truth in lies.
I remember the ocean
Opening it azure door limitlessness
Gasping for breath, drowning in hope
I am swimming far from shore
Fleeing borders, fences
Solid ground, the befouled
Around the harbor of doubt
Until the undertow of memory
Pulls me back to reality
Back to the beauty of agony
Of pain
Of home.
Alone, I return to the forest
Finding everything
In nothing.

1998

"March Snowstorm in the City"

Clouds Splitting
Hurling, swirling snowflaked insults
Without pity
On this already injured city
Walking people walk on, talk on
Live on, give on
Arrive on time
Because they have to.
Enduring closed doors, disprespect, neglect
Carrying their groceries, their babies
Their burdens
Shuddering in the cold, muttering
Inaudible curses at the wind.

March 1999

"The Dam"

Why do we build dams?
Even when they yield no more power
Even when they reduce the delta
That once provided so much
To a trickle.

A woman in the city spends her life
Working, raising her children
Her grandchildren
Providing.
But when she is not honored
And works so hard
That she can never find time for nourishment
And eats fast food and chips
Her arteries clog
Until she collapses one day
On an empty bus
Late one night
On her way home from work.

A family in Mexico finds no fish
Because a river has been damned
The arteries of the Earth
Clogged
So Las Vegas can have green lawns
And Phoenix can have air conditioning.
They will soon move to the city
To find a new life
Only to find
Less life.
The catch of the day
Replaced by fast food and chips.

Why do we build dams?
Why do we fear the flow of life?
In the blood
In the river
Of life?

July 2008

"The Department of Pureland Security"

I live in a backwards land
An upside down nation
Where Labor Day is a celebration
Of not working;
Memorial Day forgets
How horrible war really is;
And we remember the birth of Jesus, in a manger,
By buying and buying and buying
As much as we can;
Instead of celebrating
The beautiful chaos of our interdependence,
We celebrate the lonely isolation—
The Original Sin of independence—
With the war chants of the Fourth of July.

I live in a place
Where the woman singing on the train
Is insane,
And the moon
Is loony,
But the man in his car
Talking to ghosts in his ear
Is normal, because spirits are alright here,
As long as they are purchased.

In this upside down nation
We call it "conservative" to chop down forests
And replace them with shopping malls
So we can live closer to nature,
Naming them after the Indians
Whom we have exterminated.
A place where we thought

That by mispronouncing
Los Angeles and *San Rafael*
That we could all forget
That this is really *Mexico*.
This is a country,
Where a people who have been here
For 400 years,
Are called un-American.

And we called this place "home"
And invented enemies
To fear
To make it appear so.
And when they acted the part
And brought it back
Home, we were taken aback, shocked, and awed,
And invented an inside out institution called the "Department of Homeland
  Security"
To protect us from the demons
We made, and our insecurities.
Perhaps,
We need a Department of Pureland Security
Replacing Cheney's demons with *Amhitabha*,
Fearful rhetoric, with boundless radiance.
How many engineers
Would it take, I shout,
To figure out what the infinite looks like
Upside down and inside out?

September 1, 2008, California

"Borders"

Far before I reach the border,
Landscapes and languages begin to change.
English is spoken only occasionally;
In the dusty plains of south Texas—
A place that prides itself on its Americanness,
Not realizing
That the Spanish-speaking people
Make it so—
Mexico comes gradually,
Long before the border.
The snakes and the birds tell me, too,
That I have already reached a place far different
From the one I have left,
Even before I have gotten there.
The world we have paved
And drawn lines upon
In our fear of its vague and subtle
Grayness. Its slow fade
From one land to the next
In stark contrast to the comforting abruptness
Of guards and currency exchanges.

Do they
Consider the birds of the air...
The lilies of the field,
When they draw those lines,
Even as they hold Bibles
(Written in English) in hand?
The birds fly past those borders,
The lily-seeds find fertile soil on both sides.

We tell ourselves that the lines between nations
Are real
As if we know what the real really is.
Is it real because it exists on paper,
And in concrete walls built by men,
And in still harder, higher walls in our minds?
The snakes and birds, then,
Must not be real,
For they pass over and through with ease.
And people, in spite of our ideas,
Pass through, too,
Following the money on which we all depend
For survival.

These people must not be real, then:
Who move silently through the desert,
Searching for work from which others hide;
Who pick our vegetables and in their struggles
Make them cheaper.
We seem not to care
That they speak strange tongues
As we gorge ourselves
In the bloated supermarkets of entitlement.
Do we taste their suffering
In our grapes? Their struggles
In our greens?

In this backward world
In which borders are crossed daily,
Even on city buses,
In which money is real value
And lines on a map,

So allusive on the dusty borders of
Creation,
Are more real
Than the dust itself.

La Pesca, Mexico, 2003

"What's so Bad about Unrequited Love?"

What's so bad about unrequited love?
Love's joy comes from loving
More than being loved.

When the game is over
And the cheering stops
And we have lost or won
We realize that which we wanted so
Badly, as if to die for;
The Goal
Is meaningless.

And we look back
Seeing ourselves running, laughing, playing, crying
Alive
And knowing that we needed no goal
Only to live.

To love
To find the answer in the question
The destination in the journey
There is no beginning, but infinite endings
And no end, but infinite beginnings

I am in love, and waiting
For an occupant in my heart

I am in love
But don't yet know
With whom.

Chicago, January 1999

"What Did You Dream about, Brother?"

What did you dream about, brother
When they sliced you open
Disemboweled you
Took out organs
You barely knew you had;
When you lie there
Tubes sticking out
Drugs
Your only friend?
Did you dream of the days
When I would come to your room
And sleep on the floor beside your bed?
Did you dream of the knowing
That can only come from a brother?

What did you dream of, brother?
When strangers told you
As you lie prone
Cancer
The question for which there is no answer
Becomes the answer to every question.

I dreamt of regret
For lost years
For remembering the days
When I would come to sleep on the floor beside your bed;
For knowing, the knowing
That can only come from a brother,
But letting years get in the way;
Of intimacy.
I dreamt of the terror
Of not seeing sons grow up.

In these long, lonely days
I hope you dream of your sons:
The big one
Loving the little
And coming to sleep
On the floor beside his bed.

Oakland, February 2009

"Two Moments"

There are two moments
From my youth
That resound
Today:
Mandela
Walking proudly
Calmly
Dignified
Dignified
From prison;
And the burning streets of L.A.
After the Rodney King verdict.

Today:
Barack Obama, a Black Man,
With a Muslim name
President of the United States of America.
Bitter Africaaners
Of Middle America
May lament,
And perhaps
The revolution some of us hope for
Will not come
But we must, for a moment,
Pause to see not how much a single man can change
But how he can reflect the change that has already happened.

:and here in Oakland, California
A young man named Oscar Grant,
Unarmed and handcuffed
Executed on a train platform
And the streets of Oakland burn.

I see Rodney King
Defenseless and prone
Beaten
As I watch the young man
—a boy, really, but a father, too—
Murdered
I still can hear the soft Jamaican accent on the radio
On that firey night in 1991,
Dedicating a song of revolution
To Rodney King.

I hear too
Then as now,
How pointless it is to destroy property
In response to tragedy.
Unfortunate comparisons made
To blood spilt at the hands of police
To broken windows and burned cars.
I suppose there is truth in the critique of the rioters,
But I also know something greater:
I have seen Hell.
And it is neither dark nor aflame,
Nor do demons torture its inhabitants.
Hell is the moment when a human being loses the ability to lament life's
        sorrows,
And to become enraged at injustice.

Those fires,
In L.A. as in Oakland and Soweto,
Are not Hell,
But humanity's sad yearning to escape it.

And perhaps others, less oppressed but no less damned,
Have heard those cries, and
Years later,
Obama walked out on that stage
As Mandela walked free,
And a world rejoiced.

January 2009, Oakland

"Behind the Two Inch Glass"

"Where you going?" the officer said gruffly.

"Division six," I answered blankly.

The officer said nothing. He looked over my documents. He found no reason to deny my entry.

"You can't enter with this," said the woman to my side who had been searching my bag, holding up an aerosol can.

I took my bag and went back to my car, where I left everything that would prevent me from entering. I returned in a few moments, showed them my identification card, resubmitted to a search. The officer patted me down after I passed through the metal detector.

"To the right and out the door," he told me.

This is like entering a foreign country, I thought as I walked down the dark corridor. *No, this is more difficult than that. It is like entering a foreign world. It is inside of the world we know, hidden.*

The hallway led to a door to a courtyard. Not knowing where I was going, I entered the first open door I encountered.

The room was poorly lit and dingy. There were a dozen people sitting in plastic chairs nailed to the floor in neat rows. They did not talk, or read; they stared straight ahead, blankly and sadly, all of them. A woman in uniform sat behind a gate. I could barely see her in the drab and dirty darkness. She asked me whom I had come to see.

"Corinthians Dion Bell," I answered.

The woman shuffled some papers. "Have a seat," she said. "Wait for his name to be called."

I sat down among the others. They were a depressing bunch: mothers and fathers; wives and brothers. They had all come to see someone they loved who was incarcerated. Their faces were as gray and gloomy as the room.

I waited for about a forty-five minutes. His name was the first to be called. They opened a heavy and terrifying iron gate to let me enter. I saw Dion to my left as I was led to another room. My identification was scrutinized again. Finally, I was allowed into the visitation room. Dion sat behind two-inch, bulletproof glass, the kind found in hole-in-the-wall fast food places in the ghetto. He was smiling, surprised to see me. His hair had been cut short – he had had long dreadlocks the last time I had seen him, perhaps a month ago. He looked healthy and strong. He had been eating better there than he ever did when he was free.

In order to talk, we had to put our mouths and ears close to the glass and speak loudly. We made small talk at first. He told me had been doing well, he was in good health. In time, more visitors entered, each shouting into the tiny holes in the two-inch glass. It became noisy and nearly impossible to hear.

I told him, after about a half hour, that I had to leave. I wouldn't see him for a while, for I was leaving the country next week. I told him I would be in Asia. He smiled. I was not sure if he even knew where Asia was; and even if he did know, it was so far beyond his world that it did not matter. It might as well have been the moon.

Dion put his hand up to the glass. I put mine up too, mirroring his. We imagined they touched.

"Somebody killed my Moms," he said. "They think I did it."

I had known Dion for several years before he was arrested for the murder of his mother. As a student at the University of Chicago, in Hyde Park, I would see Dion wandering the streets. In time, I came to know him; he became a part of my circle of friends.

Hyde Park was one of the South Side's most affluent and integrated neighborhoods. Dion came to escape the violence of his own neighborhood. There were times when he heard the gunshots on his way home and turned around to sleep in the park; other times he was robbed.

Dion's home fluctuated between the streets and his mother's place. Sometimes he preferred homelessness: his mother was plagued by addiction; his neighborhood was gang-ridden; and his mother's home was rat-infested and unwelcoming. But he harbored no bitterness toward his mother. "She ain't too strong," he had told me once. It was the closest he had come to criticizing his mother in my presence, but it was said with affection. It was an explanation for his mother's problems, an excuse, not a condemnation.

Dion had little formal education and few prospects for employment. Often he came by hungry – we tried to give him what we could. He got a job selling "Streetwise", a newspaper sold by Chicago's homeless. He sold incense and oils. He was arrested a few times for selling the latter without a license. He would have had to stop eating for several days to afford such a license.

And Dion walked. Through Chicago's harsh and bitter winter, he walked; he walked through Chicago's brutal and violent neighborhoods. Dion crossed borders in Chicago: from one gang territory to another; and from his own poor, black neighborhood to the white and black-middle-class neighborhood of Hyde Park. Dion had nothing, but his feet; his only gift, it seemed, was his ability to walk those forbidding streets freely.

A few months before I was to leave Chicago, and America, a friend received a knock on his door. It was the police. They asked him if he knew a man named Corinthians Dion Bell. He wasn't sure. None of us had ever known him by any other name than "Dion". But he figured out who it was.

A few nights ago, Dion's mother had been stabbed to death, they told him. Dion had been arrested.

It was Dion who had found his mother covered in blood. It was no single stab wound that had killed her, but a multitude, too many to count. I have thought about how I would have responded if I had been in Dion's situation. My imagination has come up with nothing.

In shock, in horror, Dion did nothing at first. When he regained his composure, he took the money in his mother's house and left. Later, he called the police.

The police have said that the money was the motive for the crime; that Dion killed his own mother to steal from her. But of course, the truth is always deeper than appearances; or, rather, the truth is shallower. The truth is as shallow as a man's clothes and skin. Dion was poor and uneducated, with little chance to defend himself successfully in court; he was big and dark-skinned, fitting society's image of a criminal, a murderer.

I had broken bread with Dion. He had been to my home. I could never have known his innermost thoughts, the depths of his soul. But I knew him as more than his clothes and his skin. He was not a shadow, to me, drifting namelessly through the city streets. He was human…

We stood up, for a moment, facing one another. The windowless visitation room was crowded now. On both sides of the divide, mouths and ears were pressed against the two-inch glass. The small room was filled with noise. I was sure no one could hear anything that was said. I had stopped trying.

We said goodbye to each other – this is the word that does not need to be heard to be understood – and I left. As I left the building, the guard was arguing with a Mexican kid about his hat. Hats, which represented gang affiliation in Chicago, were not allowed.

The August sun shone brightly as I walked away, toward my car. There had been no windows inside.

I walked away not only from the Cook County Jail, but also from the darkness, from Chicago, from attachment, from limitation. I was free. I could leave. My imminent departure intensified, in my own mind, the cruelty of Dion's incarceration.

I would cross so many borders. Most people I knew in Chicago, most people I would encounter on my journey, would never cross an international border in their lives.

And there were other borders, more subtle but no less real, that I would be privileged to cross.

It did not occur to me then that Dion's existence had always been about crossing borders. He had spent his time with privileged University students. He had walked.

But there, as I got into my car and drove off, I felt the impassibility of the borders of his world now. The two-inch glass did not move. He had no passport, no way to move on, to continue his walk.

As I began my journey, in which I would seldom cease to move, Dion remained static in my mind, always staring out at me, through the two-inch glass.[3]

---

3 [∞] After spending a year and a half in Cook County Jail, during which time he was drugged by the prison authorities to justify the claim that he had killed his mother because he was "crazy", Dion was completely exonerated and released, thanks in large part to friends who helped secure free legal representation. He recently settled with the city of Chicago for a large sum of money.

Summer 2000

SECTION II
Purgatorio

Io ritornai da la santissim'onda
Rifatto sì, come piante novelle
Rinovellate di novella fronda
Puro e disposto a salire a le stelle.[4∞]

Dante, *Purgatorio*, Canto xxxiii, 142-145[5]

4 ∞ "I returned from the holiest wave/ remade, like new trees/ renewed of new foliage,/ pure and ready to climb to the stars." [Translation mine]
5   Dante Alighieri, *The Purgatorio of Dante Alighieri* (New York: J.M. Dent and Sons, 1952) p.428

Purgatorio: The Journey around the World

This dream I have
Standing
In this moment,
At the birth canal,
the alembic,
I realize the eschaton
Today
In this dream
Universe
Giving birth
through
the chaotic matrix
womb of past and future
Heaven and Earth
There is beauty in this bloody moment
In this pregnant moment
Birthing
Birthing
The perfectly fallen flesh
Of humanity
Blood and bone
And stardust and love
Searching for mother's breast
Looking up
At God
At mother
At the stars.

"On Leaving"

Leaving
Whether it is from the womb,
From this life
Or one of the stops along the way
Is the most intense form of experience
To leave is to relive years
In an instant
To laugh and cry at once
It is to become brave and courageous
Facing the unknown
And a shameful coward
Running from home.
It is to be infinitely hopeful as the opportunity
Of creation presents itself
And it is to resigned to the limitations
Of the single life
Of a single soul.
Seldom have I felt so alive
As when I have left a place,
A life,
A loved one.

1999

"Waiting"

Waiting
For a bus
In the barren months of Chicago's cold south side
Waiting without regard for the season
Gray streets stretching uniformly, straightly
Daley's rigid design
Without regard for nature's chaotic birthing
Crackling brown leaves mingle in the cold air—
"The hawk" is out—
With brownbags that had once clothed the medicines of alienation
And despair
Awash in thoughtless thoughts
My mind wanders
Wonders when the bus will come
The rain will stop
When the crime rate will drop
Wanders through wonders unthought, unseen
A dream in living color
A life on a black and white screen
Still
Waiting
To move
My mind thinks nothing washing
My burning heart
Waiting for the love that burns
Away
The separation of mind and me
Of city and place
Of journey and the bus schedule.
Waiting to love
The wait.

Chicago, 1999

"Africa"

I have no idea why I went to Africa. There were many reasons I could give, but none would be sufficient, or completely honest. In truth, it mostly had to do with the stories that swirled around in my blood, waiting to find the space in which to be given birth. Whatever the reason, I am amazed to ponder the fact that, 60,000 years after leaving her, I returned to write these words.

She seemed to me to be as far away as one could get. And that was surely what I sought. It was not so much a looking-for-something as a running away—running away from the comfort of the modern world, from that with which I was most familiar. I rode on the clouds in a mighty plane, tossing my books down into the Big Sea, unaware that in those depths ghosts of the Middle Passage were passing silently below.

I woke up each day at dawn with the cows, their normal docility interrupted by the agony of being milked. Momentarily, the workers would come, the women singing, the men laughing, the sweet smell of cow dung, morning tea and Eucalyptus—they, like other invasive colonies, had been brought in by foreign aid workers to control soil erosion, but greedily sucked the moisture from the earth—these smells wafting into our tin-roofed hut. The morning mist gently burned away, leaving a cool dew in the grass. I would sit outside with my fruit, looking out across the misty valley, toward Mozambique in the East. The mist seemed to come from there, although I knew it did not. I often wondered if this were the same mist Moses had seen, many years before. His had been a mist that had called him away from Africa. This mist seemed to call me back.

I would walk down to the main road early each day past a small preschool. The children knew me—there were few whites in the area—and would call out my name mellifluously as they played: "Good morning, Ted-deeeeeeee!"

I answered them in Shona: "*Mangwanani.*"

This never failed to make them laugh. Every morning I paused to look at the huge mural on the side of the school, with the Shona proverb written on it:

MWANA NDI AMAI
"The child is the mother"

My days in Africa were spent walking. My partner, Maxwell, and I were given the task of teaching groups of women to read and write. It was absurd, really. These women were often much older. They had raised children and survived wars. They grew enough food out of the parched, dusty, rocky earth to feed large families without the benefit of state welfare, irrigation or chemicals.

Their umbilical chords were buried in the African soil. And I had come to teach *them*.

Maxwell had left school in the eighth grade when his parents had died. I never asked how. But he was as knowledgeable as his bosses. And far wiser.

"Africa has many problems," he told me, "but forgetting is not one of them."

During the second to last week I worked in Zimbabwe the price of bread tripled overnight. There were strikes and riots in the cities. Mugabe was condemned by the West. The West was condemned by Mugabe. In the bush, the earth cracked in the dry air as the sun continued to beam down, day after rainless day.

The Baobab trees were unmoved.

Mozambique had finally gotten hold of me and I headed across the border. There was little there but dust. One-legged land mine victims begged on the side of the road alongside children, mumbling the only English word they knew: "please." There were no buses, so I had to hitchhike. I climbed into the back of a flatbed truck and rode from the mountains of Manicaland down into the coastal plains. Ragged men from this land—"the poorest nation on Earth"—smiled and shared their fruit when I told them I was an American.

The Africa I sought is perhaps the most terrifying place imaginable the modern human. It represents a past that is neither Edenic nor savage. The elusive moment of creation never happened. We were always being created, and still are. But it was in those rolling savannahs and among the great predators that we emerged. Our minds developed to find new ways to capture our prey and elude our predators; our legs grew long and straight to walk long distances across those plains. The grasses and the cats and the herds of Africa gave birth to us. Indeed, they are not much different from us at all. It is insufficient to say we came from mere dust, just as it is insufficient to say we were created by the gods from above.

The dust itself is divine.

On my final night in Mozambique, I left the bar late at night to find that a storm had come in from the sea, the first rain I had seen in months. My flimsy little tent had filled with water. I took what I could salvage out of the tent and went to the only sheltered place still open, the bathroom next to the bar.

And finally, in a dark bathroom, in the poorest country on Earth, it happened. I remembered, at that moment, through the rain dripping through the leaky ceiling, blended with my own tears, telling my own, unborn child: *"You are from Africa."*

And after 60,000 years of gestation, I gave birth to a story, my story. For the first time, I began to write for no other reason than the joy of feeling I must.

I wrote the following:

I have no idea why I went to Africa. There were many reasons I could give, none would be sufficient, or completely honest. In truth, it mostly had to do with the stories that swirled around in my blood, waiting to find the space in which to be given birth. Whatever the reason, I am amazed to ponder the fact that, 60,000 years after leaving her, I returned to write these words…

Mozambique, 1998

"The Wayfarer"

"We are all wayfarers. . . for there is no end to wayfaring."
　　Ibn Al-Arabi

I arrived in darkness. From one vast, empty, black infinity to another, I arrived. In the Pacific, like nowhere else in the world, the sea and the sky are mirrors. One emptiness reflecting the other, interrupted only by islands and stars, stars and islands so much the same. At night, the sameness and smallness is accentuated by the black emptiness of sea and sky.

I arrived tearfully and alone, in a smallish, raucous plane of Samoans, I the only foreigner. It took exactly one day, one empty sea, one empty sky, for my bravery to abate. I was alone, afraid.

Looking out the window, there was only blackness. Nothing. So I waited, watching the Samoans laugh and talk, happy to almost be home, back from a trip (to see relatives, probably) to the big city, Honolulu.

We landed, finally. I had been traveling all day, from Chicago to Honolulu, Honolulu to Tutuila, one of the largest planets in the Samoan solar system, in the galaxy of the Pacific.

The islands of the Pacific are so small, so seemingly insignificant, that for thousands of years people have looked up to the great mirror in the sky to find themselves. It was not with any consideration of ancient Polynesian navigators that I first looked upwards when I stepped off the plane; I was simply compelled to do so because I hadn't been able to find this little island from the window of the plane. I felt like I was landing nowhere; it was too dark.

I looked up, looking for light, looking for God.

"Fathers and Sons in Vietnam"

[For My Father and Tony, and all the other survivors of the American War in Vietnam]

I leave Ho Chi Min City on the overnight train,
up the coast, to Danang City,
in central Vietnam.
As we pass by lush jungles and pristine beaches
forests still struggling to grow back
from the chemicals dropped
by American jets,
I share a cabin with an aged father
and his son.
The father is dying.
The son wipes the father's chin tenderly
when he coughs,
carries him to the bathroom,
massages him.
There is no nursing home in
Vietnam, where each is condemned and privileged
to watch his parents die,
condemned and privileged to watch his children
watch him die.

They speak no English,
but we begin to become friends.
A younger brother comes from third-class—
they could only afford two second-class seats—
sharing his fruit with me.
They get off before me.
I watch as they meet their family outside
point to me and wave and laugh.
The father, for the first time,
breaks his stoic expression
and smiles.

We, the Americans,
did so much harm to this country.
And we did so much harm to our selves in the process.
But in this Buddhist land
they understand
how in harming others
we really hurt ourselves,
know we have suffered for our presence there,
suffering passed from husband to wife,
father to son,
brother to brother.
Not only those who came to Vietnam felt its pain.

My father served in Vietnam.
I do not know what effect it had on him:
he did not become homeless,
or a drug addict;
he seldom spoke of it,
and then, only in superficial ways:
the spicy food, the breathtaking landscape,
his boat.
And I am too young to remember the war.
But Vietnam still has a resonance with me,
a special place in my imagination.
As much as I would like to deny it,
my own identity is connected to the American experience in Vietnam.
So this, for me, is a homecoming of sorts.

The father will soon die,
As his sons and his wife rub his legs and gently pat his head,
In the stifling Vietnamese heat,
With a cold, damp cloth.

But he will remain with the family
In the sons
Who are privileged to watch him die.

Vietnam, 2000

"Tibet is Ours"

To travel the world as an American in the twenty first century
is like traveling the Mediterranean in the first century as a Roman.
Americans are neither revered nor despised,
but they are always paid attention to.

I have seen few places as beautiful
as the southern Chinese countryside,
ride over the rolling, moist, green plains of rice patties,
abruptly interrupted by rocky mountains,
emerging with such immediacy from the fields that—
if I did not know better—
I'd have thought they had been driven straight into the ground
by God's own hand.
I ride through tiny villages,
unchanged for centuries,
past people living in homes carved out of caves.
Over sleepy, serene rivers, I ride.

I spend all of my days in Yangshuo this way.
Riding.
Occasionally I divert to walk up a mountain or explore a cave.
In the evening, I walk through town,
talking to a fellow foreigner,
but mostly keeping to myself.
I have little to say to the foreigners I meet;
aloof, reticent, silent, and happy,
I eat my dinner alone each evening,
doing battle with my chopsticks.

I leave Yangshuo and head north
on an overnight train to Zhengzhou,
looking for a more "authentic" China.

It is a city of smog, in which,
Even on a clear day,
The sun is obscured.
A city of xenophobia
And distrustful stares.

The train is different.
The Chinese make themselves at home on the train,
dressing and undressing,
eating, drinking and laughing.
A group of women approach me.
When they discover that I am alone
and speak no Chinese, they become concerned.
Hwang, who speaks more English than the rest,
Decides to be my guide.
Tall, serious, plain-looking with very crooked teeth
she does not speak enough English
for me to truly figure out why she is so kind to me.
She is a patriot, a nationalist, and warns me,
when I tell her that I am going to Tibet,
"Tibet is ours."

I continue on to the dusty, desperate Tibetan Plateau.
It is in Tibet, this vast, empty place,
that I thought I would become empty.
Tibet contrasts China in every way:
As I ride the small bus across the stark countryside,
I squint in the brilliant sunshine.
There are no clouds in the sky,
not even small, white, rainless ones.
It reminds me of the dry season in Africa
Much more than the smog and pollution of China

Where it was possible to look straight at the sun
Even on a "clear" day.
The air is cool,
but I can feel our proximity to the sun.

In the clear, cool air of Tibet,
I nearly die from lack of oxygen.
My head wrapped in bloody bandages now
From an altitude-sickness-induced fall,
I traverse the great plateau
From Lhasa to the foot of Everest
To the little town of Tashi Dzom
Where I drink beer with Tibetans
And an Italian friend
And in the evening
The children come out into the street
To sing and dance
In the cold moonlight
Marveling at the stars
Thanking God and ourselves—our own Buddha Nature
Under the shadow of Everest.

Tibet 2000

"At a Train Station in India"

I.
At a train station, somewhere
Anywhere
in India
mobs of people everywhere,
sitting, smoking bidis, staring blankly.
Dogs fight in front of the entrance.
A cow wanders unmolested through the interior,
dropping dung on the floor, mooing loudly.
A boy paces across the platform,
past the men urinating onto the tracks,
past the rows and rows of families
lined up in as orderly a manner as anything else I would encounter in India—
this is where they will sleep tonight—
with his tea kettle, calling out rhythmically
the unofficial anthem of India:
"Cha – chaaaiiii."

II.
The ride to Varanasi is short.
I sit by the window
and watch the uninteresting scenery of the Ganga plain,
watch the people defecate in their fields.
A little boy with no legs scurries down the isle,
sweeping the garbage off the floor.
His head remains down,
conveying his diligence,
his total consumption by his task,
his humility, his inferiority.
He sweeps quickly,
only looking up to ask for money.
The chai man steps over him.
"Cha-chaaaaiiii!"

III.
On a train from Varanasi to Calcutta,
There are two people sleeping in my bunk,
refugees from overcrowded third-class.
I show another passenger my ticket—
I encounter no train workers during the whole ride—
and he helps me get them to move aside.
The long ride is made worse
by minor stomach problems.
I ride with a family of rough, friendly Kashmiris.
After nearly twenty-four hours, I arrive in Calcutta.

IV.
Calcutta is the city of my dreams.
As much as I have dreamt of ancient ruins,
empty beaches and mountaintops,
I have dreamt of Calcutta.
An Aussie in Apia—a man who made his living installing ATMs in third world
countries—
once told me it was the worst place on Earth.
The poverty of Calcutta captured my imagination,
the only place on Earth
where rickshaws are still pulled
by men on foot rather than bicycles;
a place where people live on the street,
not solitary individuals,
but entire families.
And they live there with such dignity!
They clean their dishes;
bathe, with soap, in their underwear on the corner.
Calcutta is indeed the city of my dreams.

V.
There is something about Indian poverty
that makes it seem worse than any other.
India's poverty, like everything else there,
is *more*.
More of everything.
The poor of India are not only poor,
they lie in the street,
bleeding and dying.
They are not merely sick;
they are lepers.

VI.
As I set out one morning in search of work,
there are men in their underwear,
lathering their bodies with soap,
bathing on the corner.
Women wash clothes and dishes.
A leper tugs at my sleeve;
I give him some change.
Another man lay on the corner on his back, moaning,
his body covered with boils.
There is a small cup next to him.
I cringe as I step over him,
and cringe again,
ashamed at my discomfort.

VII.
Further along a group of children
play on a pile of garbage
Dirty, but somehow impervious
to the stench,

seem somehow to float above it.
They smile.
Theirs is not the expectant smile
of the rickshaw driver,
but the smile of pure joy.
I remember there is a slum in Calcutta called "The City of Joy".
I walk through the slums,
past the smells.
The smells of India!
Bidis and incense,
cow dung and curry,
Pictures of the place are always insufficient
because they cannot capture its smell.

VIII.
I ride on to the Taj Mahal,
which the great Indian poet Tagore
called a great teardrop.
Indeed, it does look like a giant tear,
falling up,
from the tormented land, into the endless, burdenless sky.
And India itself recalls a giant teardrop,
falling slowly from the Himalayas into the Indian Ocean,
the crying earth matching a crying, dying people,
flowing from the confusion of this land,
where sense and order are always sought but never attained,
into the great, simple ocean,
where salt and water and life do not feel the need to be
separated, ordered, understood.
I sit peacefully and write in the shadow of the Taj Mahal,
waiting until it is time to return to the train station.

IX.
Indian tea is not merely chai,
But *masala* chai
Mixed.
I ride on to Haridwar to study with a Sadhu
Who teaches me little,
But asks me often for money.
He is sick
From drinking holy Ganga water
"God is Ganga," he says.
Haridwar is a holy city.
Each night, the people come down to the Ganga
at the *Hari-Ki-Pairi* Ghat
and leave tiny boats with candles floating down the river,
candles carrying wishes.
I am not sure,
but I guess the wish rests in the flames.
If the candle reaches the sea,
the wish is fulfilled.
I stare at the army of wishes,
doubting any will make it.
I think of all that has been put in the river:
Dead bodies and garbage and wishes.
Plastic bags float alongside holy candles
in this holiest of rivers.
It is purely Indian, like chai:
Masala.

India, 2000

"At the Edge"

In the Red Sea,
The most barren of landscapes
Meets a Universe of color,
The ragged, rugged peeks of the Sinai,
Meet the depths of the Red Sea reefs,
Where a swimmer,
A man,
Approaches the edge,
And moves from the ease,
Of two-foot-deep wading
To the depths of the abyss.
He pauses
For a moment,
Fearful of the depths,
Until he sees
That the beauty of the reefs
Lies beyond the edge
And the sea supports him just the same
In the depths
As in the shallows.

I stand here
Poised at the precipice
Of tomorrow.
The ape peering out from the forest;
The polar bear poised to dive into the sea
Even as his icy home melts;
The infant
Entering the birth canal;
The mother,
Awaiting motherhood.

To be alive,
Is to live
At the edge.
To be at the edge
Is to give birth
To each moment
In this pregnant world;
Standing at the high cliffs,
Above the churning,
Dancing,
Salty Sea,
Giving birth
Each moment
Pregnant with tomorrow
At the edge,
Of unknowing.

September 2008, California

"Among the Godwrestlers"

By the rivers of Babylon
We sat and wept
When we remembered Zion.

"We need this rain," the Israeli tells me,
"We give all our water to the fucking Arabs,"
I simply look at him
And nod
And walk on
Through the city of Jerusalem
The empty city—the tourists have been scared off—
to which I have come from the
Great empty Jordanian deserts
Where I wept at the intimate immensity of the stars;
Across the teeming kaleidoscopic world of the Red Sea reefs;
And through the Spartan landscapes of the Sinai,
The barren vistas that revealed to Moses,
As much as any bush,
The burning of his heart;
And finally, across the Gaza strip, in a military vehicle
Peeking out of the little slits
At the barrenness,
Protected by steel
And American guns
And lonely fences
Until I reached Israel
The Land of the Godwrestlers
A land of Milk and honey
And American money
Of manicured lawns
Of deserts made alive
Of lives made as barren
As the desert.

After years in the wilderness
They made the bargain

That most of us made
Many years before:
To turn the plowshares
Of the wayfarer
Of the Godwrestler
Into the swords of the nation state.
To eat from the Tree
of the Knowledge of Good and Evil
that gave us the capacity to make *distinctions*—
between ourselves and others,
between right and wrong.
To build fences.

Isra-el, the Godwrestlers.
The masters of return—
baal teshuvim—
realize that all is God, nothing
no one separate from anything or anyone else.
The wrestling never ends.
The paradox never resolved.
The fruit of the tree promises an illusion.
To return to paradise,
embrace the paradox.

My father was a wandering Aramean...
Sometimes, we must become wanderers ourselves
to remember that since we first emerged
on the African Savannahs millennia ago,
we have been wayfarers.
Some of us can never cross those fences
That I so casually passed by.
Some remain on our own Nebo

Peering into the future,
While others
cross those borders
And settle down
Within the oppressive and fleeting safety
Of the Nation State.
My father, the wanderer, the wayfarer,
Still lives
In me,
Reminding me
That I too was once an outsider
Looking in.

2001, Jerusalem

"At the Confluence of Longing and Belonging"

A man and woman met
at the confluence
of longing and belonging.
How do I know when I'm in love?
He asked
And she answered
As only a mother can.
The pain, she said.
The pain.

Is there a difference between one kind of love
and another?
At what point
Do we know if our feelings
Are merely the fleeting glance of knowing eyes;
The touch of identical fingertips,
Souls disparate.
Ephemeral
Or, is it the inlovingness that never leaves
Even when it has no hope
Or even desire of being requited?
The kind that remains imprinted on the soul,
Its recipient forever a part of who we are.
Its painful joy—
Or joyful pain—
What
We are;
Our emotional, spiritual
Flesh.

Anyone who has loved this way
This permanent way
Bears its scars
Some learn to embrace them

Like war heroes do
Others cover them
In hats and scarves and longsleeves.
In smiling masks.

But in the end
Scars are all we are left with.
Sex and marriage and friendship ends.
Life ends.
Love, if it is the right kind,
Leaves a scar on the soul than can endure,
An agonizing, exposing cross to bear
But it is better to carry it
Than to be the cross of another
In the end
It leaves you reborn
With scars never to be washed away, even in death.

Two rivers meet here
One, the river of belonging, flows from our past
Reminding us of who we are
That we have been birthed in love
Reminding us that we need to look nowhere to find it
Another, the river of longing, flows from this moment
Into the possibility of the future
The ever-not-quite-ness of now.
Here, in the heart,
At the confluence of longing and belonging,
At the chaotic matrix of each moment,
Awe-some and Awe-ful,
Terrific and Terrible,
Love is born.

Chicago, 1999

"Christmas in New York"

In a dark, quiet corner
Amid the blackness of the season of light
Lonesome in a crowd of millions
Sipping hopeful wine, in a hopeless time.

I wonder how many more dreams will die
Before we dance the dance of resurrection.
I know now, how chaotic Jerusalem must have been
On that dark, holy night, many years ago.

In this dark season of light
Christmas, holy profundity
The time of the birth of God
The time of the crying, laughing baby
Born in the soul of millions
In every dark, quiet corner,
Of New York City, at Christmas.

New York, 2004

"Venice"

I wander into Venice as a specter,
floating through the twisted streets
of that romantic, sinking city
whose glory days have long since passed.
It seems the perfect place to be,
a place in which one can peer into both past—
the glorious Venician empire—
and future—
the future that a place like New Orleans can look forward to,
as a faded reminder of humanity's ephemeral presence
on a piece of land sinking into the sea.
I have given birth to my nakedness in the Mediterranean.
It is cold, and I wrap myself in a Pakistani shawl,
Intensifying my outsider-ness,
stopping only occasionally for a glass of wine.
Everywhere I go I am haunted by ghosts,
see them in the gelato shops and churches and places I have visited.
It is *Carnivale*
(What is it about drowning cities and Carnival?)
the narrow streets of Venice filled with masks.
I must leave this place, I think.
There are too many memories in Venice.
I am a traveler.
I have no memory, only the road.
There are so many endings,
but the beginnings still seem so far away,
in a future that does not yet seem real.

I return to Rome on an overnight train,
sharing a sleeper car with two couples:
I sleep on the top bunk.
The couples, so they can see one another's eyes as they lay down, I suppose,
sit across from one another.
There is an empty seat across from me.

Italy, February 2001

"Paris"

It is here that the end begins.

Here, in gray, gay, lonely Paris, I sense, for the first time, that my journey is ending. I am neither happy nor sad. I am nothing. Empty. For this journey was, in many ways, an emptying.

Is this where my soul begins to be filled up again? Will God pour from her mighty carafe wine or water, nectar or oil? I do not see whence this renewal will come. I feel so far away from anything and everything.

I have seen so many places, been so many things. I have crossed borders into the depths of my own heart that I did not know existed. I have crossed mountains, deserts and jungles. I have crossed borders so seldom crossed. I walk through these cold, broad streets wearily—my feet hurt from the months of walking; my tooth aches from time to time; I am thin and bald; there is a scar over my right eye—but I feel as though I could keep moving forever. I realize that as difficult as traveling can be, it can be more difficult to stop.

I have been everything in the eyes of those I have encountered: strange and exotic; a crook and a cheat; annoying and selfish and suspicious. I have been grotesque. All that I have feared and abhorred on the faces of those I encountered, I have been.

And now I begin my descent from the thin air and barren ground of the stark mountaintop. I am transported, in my mind, to Mt. Sinai, looking across the Sinai, seeing nothing but nothingness, rock upon dry, barren rock. I am there. Here in the café and at the bread shop, listening to jazz and hip hop, I am atop the lonely mountain. I am the mountain – barren and dry and empty. I scarcely remember the landscape to which I will return, do not know if it will still feel like home.

I will soon return to the place—America, Chicago—whence I came. This journey, like all journeys, will be a circle, beginning and ending at the same point, so different and so much the same.

Paris, March 2001

SECTION III

Paradiso

All'alta fantasia qui mancò possa;
Ma già volgeva il mio disiro e il velle,
Sì come rota ch'egualmente è mossa,
L'amor che move il sole e l'altre stelle.[6]

Dante, *Paradiso*, Canto xxxiii, 142-145[7]

---

6   "Here the power of the high fantasy was lost;/ but already my desire and will were rolled/ like a wheel that moves equally/ by the love that moves the sun and the other stars."

7   Dante Alighieri, *The Paradiso of Dante Alighieri* (London: J.M. Dent and Sons, 1954) p.408

Paradiso: The Journey of the Imagination

This dream we had
Of a future not built
By engineers
But by poets
Of a journey not on a straight road
Of lines and plans
But of expansion
Into possibility
The vastness of the Imagination
Long ago
We sat around the fires
Under those stars
Burning birthing
Dreams stories
And around those same stars, danced planets
Dreaming of us.
There was fire that burned from the very start
The fire next time will burn on in my heart
Deep in the heavens is the inferno of the past
Deep in the future is the inferno of the past
Deep in my heart is the possibility of paradise
The paradise of possibility
Dreams of the stars born in my heart
Dreams of possibility born in the stars.

"The Return"

Iland in Chicago after an uneventful flight. I wait in a long line at customs and immigration. They give me no trouble, much to my surprise. I expected more questions, more suspicion because of my appearance—I look *Muslim*, like a *terrorist*—and the strange stamps on my passport. The officer barely looks at my passport. He notices my hat. "Tibet?" he says.

I smile and nod.

There is a long wait for my bag. I am nervous, ostensibly because of my bag, but probably, subconsciously, because I am home. The Mexican airport workers argue in broken English with the Indian passengers whose English is even more broken. This is America, I remember. America is many places.

The bag comes, finally, and I walk out of the airport, alone. I stand on the sidewalk, looking, waiting for nothing-in-particular. It is freezing. I have not felt such cold in a long time. I will have to get some warmer clothes. I am in Chicago again.

I ride the "el" train from north to south, from the hotels of O'Hare International Airport, downtown—under downtown, in the subway—to the South Side. The "el" follows the Dan Ryan Expressway, bisecting the South Side. The projects tower over us to the east. I am on the border between the working class white neighborhoods to the west and the ghettos and projects to the east. I, who have crossed so many borders, now ride on one.

An old woman stands up in the front of the car. She is slightly bent, but confident, buoyant and cheerful. Her skin is dark and wrinkled. "Praise the Lord," she shouts as she begins her sermon. "Who here knows Jesus?" she asks.

We are silent.

"I have been to the deepest, darkest valleys," she continues. "In my life, I have known so much despair. Who here has known despair in they life?"

She pauses. Only the grinding rails of the "el" respond. A man passes by selling socks and batteries and bootleg tapes. No one buys them.

"But each time," the old woman continues. "Each and every time, no matter how lonesome and desperate and miserable I was, Jesus was there."

The woman looks down sadly, then out the window. "Amen?" She waits for an "amen" from her congregation. She is undeterred when she does not get it. She opens her Bible and begins to read, but quickly puts it down, singing an old spiritual:

Let us cheer the weary traveler,
Cheer the weary traveler,
Along the heavenly way.

She begins to sing as we arrive at 47th Street. This is my stop. I walk across the long, cold platform alone. On the street, I wait, shivering for the bus.

We sit in silence as we ride. Where am I going? I think, realizing that I have nowhere to go. I feel the urge to get off the bus. I must get off the bus. I must walk. There must be more borders to cross.

I have crossed so many borders: borders of mountains, of deserts, of rivers, of oceans, and of guns; I have crossed borders of misunderstanding.

I get off the bus. I am alone, cold. I am home. There are boarded up storefronts. I am the only white man on this street. I am a foreigner. I walk on past the old-timers sitting on milk crates, past the baggy-pantsed boys standing idly, past women and girls with legions of children. Across the street, I see children playing in a garbage-strewn empty lot next to a dumpster. I pause to watch as they, oblivious to me, bounce on an old, dirty mattress. They bounce higher and higher, at first quite serious and competitive. But smiles creep out, then laughter. Higher they bounce. Now they are holding hands. They seem almost to touch the sky as the bounce, carried to the heavens by their laughter, before they come crashing down, embracing, out of breath and laughing on the dirty mattress, in the midst of the garbage.

I hear singing. It comes from the church next door. I hadn't noticed it was a place of worship—it lacks the grandeur of The Golden Temple, Emam Mosque, or St. Peter's Basilica. It is a tiny hole in the wall, a storefront. "House of God" is painted simply and sloppily on the front. Can that music, those voices, be coming from there? The voices grow louder; the children are bouncing again, now to the rhythm of the music. Their laughter is a song, their bounce a dance. They are worshipping their own existence.

And here, after searching the world over for enlightenment and joy and beauty, and finding more often than not only the ugliness of the world we have made, I find the beauty for which I left. My journey ends where it began; like all journeys, it was a circle, but like all journeys, the same place seems so different after being gone. It was here the whole time, at home in Chicago at its coldest and ugliest. For the greatest, most perfect, most transcendent beauty is found just then and there: in the midst of the ugliness.

I cross the street. I want to enter the church. I want to join the children, to fill my empty soul in that empty lot, to bounce and laugh and sing. But I do not, can not. I am impeded by no mountain range, no gun toting soldier. But there is a border nonetheless, one I cannot cross today.

I am crying. Down on my knees on the cold concrete, I am praying now. Crying and praying. Praying and crying. Unsure if there is any difference.

I have crossed so many borders: borders of snow-capped mountains and desert, of endless water. I have crossed borders few would cross, of the mind as well as the body. But the borders that seem most terrifying, which take us through rugged terrain and into unfamiliar places inhabited by those we have been taught to fear, are the easiest. There are places where two inches of glass provide a more impassible border than the world's highest mountains. And the borders of my heart—exposed after shedding the layers of comfort, of what-I-know and who-I-am—are the most difficult to pass of all.

I have crossed borders, so many borders.
And still, there are so many left to cross.

Chicago, March 2001

"Le Stelle"

"All truths wait in all things…
…I believe a leaf of grass is no less than the journey of the stars…"
      Walt Whitman, *Leaves of Grass*

My story begins and ends with the stars:
As a little boy, they fascinated me.
I remember looking out my window
at the nighttime sky,
although many stars
were obscured by the ambient city lights.
Perhaps I intuited, like our ancestors,
that I could find where I came from in the stars,
that the stars were my ancestors.
At the same time, the emptiness and "infinite spaces" of the Universe
    terrified me.
Years later, I would read Pascal
and recognize my own terror.
Like many in the modern world,
the search for meaning took me away from the stars.

From my room
I could look out at a tree,
Its leaves dancing on my wall
In shadows cast by moonlight
And street lights.
This moment, of beauty, is the springtime.
We are the flowers, birthing the fruit of summer's possibility.

Years later, I am on a bus in the tribal areas of western Pakistan
I am sick (some bad dates, perhaps)
Miserable overnight ride to the border of Iran
passing camel caravans and armed entourages of tribal leaders.
Bending over in pain,
Finally reaching the border village early on a frigid desert morning,
I walk out into the desert to relieve myself;
wander back into the village.
No where to go—the border does not open for several hours—

So I lay back on some burlap sacks
Filled with rice
Or some other grain
Looking up at the stars.
Remembering
It is Christmas morning.
(Christmas is low key in the tribal areas of western Pakistan)
But unlike in my childhood,
feeling not fear, but intimacy.
A few minutes later, some elders invite me into their home
For tea, and when they discover I am an American
They only laugh
And pour more tea.
Creative compassion is even more powerful
far from home, and alone.

We are, at this moment of beauty, like my daughter
putting handprints on the womb,
like the first people, painting handprints inside the caves.
We are, at this moment—this pregnant moment—at the edge of our Universe,
giving birth to ourselves, giving birth to the fruit of summer's possibility,
being born into a new womb
in which we have the capacity,
through the songs we sing and the poems we read and the stories we tell
through our Imagination
to connect to the stars, to one another
through creative compassion.
Even as autumn's long shadows cause leaves and fruit to fall
To fall.

Spring 2008

"1-2-5"

African hair-braiders call out "mees… mees"
To every woman who passes by
Muslims sell incense and oils
Jamaicans sell books
With titles like *Thug Love* and *Melanin: The Superiority of the Black Man*
Women float by in *Burqa*
Past young Dominican girls showing off their newfound curves
Garveyites shout provocatively through loudspeakers in front of pictures of
     lynchings
While across the street
Old women pass out Jehovah's Witness pamphlets
Next to Black Israelites and Five Percenters
"Newports, Newports" muttered by men on corners
Seemingly in rhythm with the African women…
One-two-five
Is a full color painting
Of the America from which
Black and white America hides
The America that one day—
When the Empire falls and the mythmakers have no more agenda
And can simply tell the story of America—
Will be born.

Harlem, 2004

"Appalachian Autumn Womb"

I drive eastward out of Upstate New York, smoking bidis.
The dull monotony of interstate gloom
turns abruptly into rural joy;
small mountains replace the small,
depressed cities of post-industrial New York.
Cows are seen more often than people.
Small farms dot the landscape
when there is a break in the roughness of the topography.
Most of the rural routes are lined with stone fences
barely visible through the tangled brush,
a reminder that people had once come here
to conquer the land,
chopping down the forests,
using the abundant rocks they found
when trying to farm
as walls.
The forest has returned,
its thickness
a testament to the strength of nature;
the presumptuousness of those walls
a testament to humanity's hubris.

I pass by tourists
Who take pictures of the landscape.
Green countryside turns to
orange, brown, and yellow.
But I enter her,
take long walks in the woods,
assaulted by the colors, above, below,
and on all sides.
I fast for days in this forest womb of ambient color,
the long Autumn shadows

and ever more barren trees
a soft reminder of the cold winter ahead,
a reminder that nature celebrates death
as well as life.

These tourists cannot see
That while the forest is pretty
From the roadside
Its true beauty
Is found within.

Appalachia 1997

"The Hills of Memory"

From the depths of the city,
I cannot but cast my eyes to the hills that envelop us.
Is it possible that I remember them
although I never saw them until I came to California?
Is it possible that I remember them so clearly,
that I cherish them like the memories of the tree
in front of the house in which I grew up, as dearly
as the memory of my mother holding me as a child?

Every hill is a memory,
and every hill has a story:
From the midst of the tumultuous city,
From the teeming flats where
only the tops are apparent;
I cannot see the depths from which they have arisen,
cannot easily recognize that they all are connected,
unless I look deeper,
toward their roots.
They can nourish me, caress me,
bringing me closer to a story far beyond my own;
or, they can serve as a boundary,
enclosing me in a prison of my own story.

If only we lived long enough,
My teacher once told me,
We would see the hills bounding across the plain
Like gazelles.
And when they burn
Or drown those mansions from their sides
They are simply tossing off riders
Like wild horses.

Is it is possible that somehow
The hills that look down upon the Oakland flats
Are not confining us at all,
But are simply passing by,
reminding us of the days when we were once them?
Is it possible that the hills of my memories
are not really mine at all?

Oakland, August 2006

"Eternal Pearl"

The full moon comes,
Every now and then,
As a reminder.
Perhaps, if we saw her in her fullness each night
We would take her for granted,
Pay less attention to the memories she brings.
And we modern people—
Especially Americans—
Are so good at forgetting.

She reminds me that there is beauty
In light that shines
Without obscuring other lights;
Reminds me of my ancestors,
Telling stories in the moonlight;
Of the rhythm of the ocean;
Of my mother's body, nourishing me.

Maybe it is the ambient light that makes us so keen to forget,
Or maybe the TVs, telephones and other technologies
Buzzing in our ears,
Distracting us,
Rendering us so easy to control.
I am grateful, however,
That none of this will ever keep her, *l'eterna margarita,*
From rising,
Full and pregnant with soft, luminous reminders
Each month.

Full Moon, September 2008

"If Only Plato Knew"

If only Plato had known
How the cave had protected his ancestors,
How his mother's womb had nourished him.
Perhaps then,
he would not have been
So eager to leave.

And even when he did,
He might have been able to see
That when we leave a womb
A cave
A world
We enter into a new one:
A cave that shelters us, contains us;
A womb that nourishes us;
And a world that we must create,
Give birth to.

If only he had known
We can never leave it all behind
That the world that nourishes our bodies
Nourishes our souls, too.

Summer 2008

"Intersubjectivity"

[Dedicated to Brian Swimme and Thomas Berry]

I walk on a cloudy day,
Like a black and white photograph
Through a city
Frozen in time
Passers by
Pass me by
Without a pause
In their cars
Steel boxes
They have mistaken
For themselves
As they scream and curse
At the other containers
Of their separate
Disparate souls
I drive, say the Cartesians, *therefore I think I am…*
Alone.

I stop to eat
At a delightfully dingy café
A tired old woman
Pours me some more coffee—
Neither kindly, nor cruelly—
For which I have not asked.
It is a gift I can never repay,
(Even with a generous tip.)
She has poured her life into mine,
And neither I nor my descendents
Will live another day
Without some subtle memory
Of this moment.

July 2008

"Parenthood"

I would put you to sleep
Rocking you
Holding you
Walking from room to room
Looking out the window
At the trees
You loved so much,
As you cried
And squirmed
In my arms.

And at last
Your eyes would grow heavy.
What a relief,
When finally
I could lay you down;
When I could let go.

But there was always a pause,
A moment,
When I realized
That what I wanted most
Was not to let you go at all,
But to hold you.

And I would,
For just a few more minutes,
Before I had
To let you go.
I looked at those trees,
As you did,
As I do now,

As I remember,
And wept silently,
Knowing, fearing
Letting you go
Forever.

Summer 2008

"The Day my Daughter was Born"

My daughter was born into a room of wise women.
She brought with her
Memories of the ancestors:
The stars in her flesh;
The seas in her tears;
Memories of mammalian compassion
When she searched for her mother's breast;
Memories of the first people
Wandering out on to the African plain,
Of painting the inside of the cave
As she did inside her womb.
She brought with her
Memories of Ellis Island, where they told her to remember no more,
And the Middle Passage, which she never could forget.

My daughter was born from a womb of boundless wisdom.
She could have shared all this, I'm sure.
But after looking up at me,
She simply cried.
Knowing one's audience, they say, is a sign of wisdom.

April 7, 2008, Oakland

"The Last Lonely Beach"

From our earliest days
The human has been the walking ape.
The ape that could stand straight
And swing her long legs
For days
Searching for nothing more
Than solitude.

Every wayfarer carries this memory
And every wanderer, bears the cross
Of the lonely oppression
Of a world too crowded
With walking apes
And not nearly enough room
For communion.

But there used to be a place
On the northern coast of Bahia
Where one could walk
Only a few miles from the town
Called *Sitio do Conde*
And sit on a beach
Alone
Under the ruins,
Of an old beach bar.

I went there to listen to the surf
And to hear the rhythm of the Earth
And Moon
Commune, with *Yamaya*.
To remember
The ocean

To remember
My wandering ancestors.

Only a few noises could be heard:
The surf
The wind
A lonely bird
And the faint sound in the distance
Of the mighty trucks
As they built the road
That would bring resorts and tourists and money and crowds.

On the walls of the old bar
A graffito was written:
YANKEE GO HOME!
I stared at the sea
Unsure if I disagreed.

Salvador da Bahia, January 2003

"The Love that Burns"

To know
What it means to be human;
To find the wisdom to become
Homo sapiens:
To live the love
That burns;
To remember,
And to dream a world
To life;
To sing songs, to write poems, to tell stories;
To taste the wind with our tongues
And to listen to the leaves;
To press our tiny hands
To the edge of our womb world;
To be amazed and terrified,
At this awesome, awful world;
To be born,
Bloody, swollen, and full of possibility.

July 2008

"When I am Old and Gray"

When I am old and gray,
When my beard hangs long,
My muscles weary,
My mind dull.
When I sit in my chair
Alone,
Pondering the soft breeze
And the old oak tree
And I know my time has come
And gone.
Even if I do not know the mysteries
Of life and death
(and I suspect I will not)
I will smile
And know
That I have found eternity
In the bloody, messy birth of my daughter,
In the dancing smile of the child;
In the tears and pain
Of falling in love
For the first terrific and terrible time;
In the joyful laughter
Of a wine filled evening;
On the back of a lorry
Racing through the bush
Of the African savannah;
In the tall grass
Waving in the moonlight,
While Orion does cartwheels across the southern sky.

And I will know
That I have found all the answers
I care to know
In the imperfect, human, moments
Of eternity.

Summer 2008

EPILOGUE

"La Nuova Commedia"

Inferno: The Journey into the Soul

Fire
I write these words
With a mind, a hand
A body
On fire
A soul is born
And at its center
Is a cosmos
Of memories
The past
Burning in my depths
A soul
A body
A Universe
Birthed in fire
Dark Matter
Is my Dark Mother,
I see her in deep in space
Burning
In my heart.
The primordial fireball
The stars,
The fire of
My ancestors
Dance around the fire
Dance around the Sun
Dance around my soul
On fire
My Ancestors,
The stars.

Purgatorio: The Journey around the World

This dream I have
Standing
In this moment,
At the birth canal,
the alembic,
I realize the eschaton
Today
In this dream
Universe
Giving birth
through
the chaotic matrix
womb of past and future
Heaven and Earth
There is beauty in this bloody moment
In this pregnant moment
Birthing
Birthing
The perfectly fallen flesh
Of humanity
Blood and bone
And stardust and love
Searching for mother's breast
Looking up
At God
At mother
At the stars.

Paradiso: The Journey of the Imagination

This dream we had
Of a future not built

By engineers
But by poets
Of a journey not on a straight road
Of lines and plans
But of expansion
Into possibility
The vastness of the Imagination
Long ago
We sat around the fires
Under those stars
Burning birthing
Dreams stories
And around those same stars, danced planets
Dreaming of us.
There was fire that burned from the very start
The fire next time will burn on in my heart
Deep in the heavens is the inferno of the past
Deep in the future is the inferno of the past
Deep in my heart is the possibility of paradise
The paradise of possibility
Dreams of the stars born in my heart
Dreams of possibility born in the stars.

February 2009

Breinigsville, PA USA
01 November 2009
226851BV00003B/3/P

9 781592 994427